Last Steam Locomotives of SPAIN & PORTUGAL

A metre-gauge CP train climbing out of the Douro Valley at Tua. The broad-gauge line can be seen in the background. E81 was one of an 1886 batch of 2-6-0Ts built by Emil Kessler of Esslingen for the *Companhia Nacional./M.J.F.*

VIA Y OBRAS 22 SECCION TALLER
RENFE

Last Steam Locomotives of SPAIN & PORTUGAL

M. J. Fox

LONDON

IAN ALLAN LTD

First published 1978

ISBN 0 7110 0698 9

Published by Ian Allan Ltd, Shepperton, Surrey; and printed in the United Kingdom by Ian Allan Printing Ltd

"To Lyn, for typing it".

Foreword

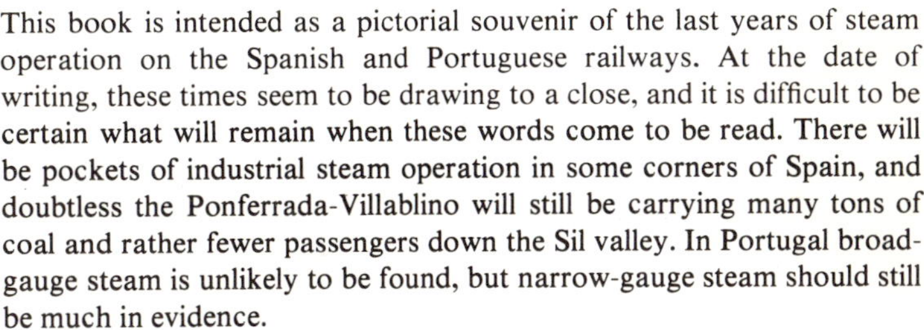

This book is intended as a pictorial souvenir of the last years of steam operation on the Spanish and Portuguese railways. At the date of writing, these times seem to be drawing to a close, and it is difficult to be certain what will remain when these words come to be read. There will be pockets of industrial steam operation in some corners of Spain, and doubtless the Ponferrada-Villablino will still be carrying many tons of coal and rather fewer passengers down the Sil valley. In Portugal broad-gauge steam is unlikely to be found, but narrow-gauge steam should still be much in evidence.

I have tried without complete success to provide a balanced selection of pictures from the different areas of the peninsula, covering the typical sights of the last twenty years. Inevitably those lines on which steam survived the longest received extra attention from the photographers, and so have yielded more material. For example on the CP I have seen virtually no pictures, except at Barreiro, from anywhere south of the Tagus. In contrast, the Douro Valley has provided an embarrassingly large selection of splendid pictures. In consequence, the photographs themselves have been the final arbiters of the balance of the subject matter.

If the geographical coverage of subjects has been somewhat uneven, that of the contributors themselves has been blatantly so. Essentially I have compiled a view of the Iberian railway scene as interpreted by visiting British enthusiasts. I hope the book will nonetheless be welcomed by readers of whatever nationality, as a reasonable attempt to portray the visual fascination of the Spanish and Portuguese railways to a steam enthusiast.

Looking at the scenes portrayed in this volume it is striking how often one or both members of the locomotive crew are visible, leaning out of the cab. This is too frequent to be chance, and I hope that some of the enginemen concerned will be able to see their pictures in times to come. This thought also reminds me that although the topic of the book is the steam locomotive it is also, by association, a tribute to the men who ran and maintained them.

May I thank all the contributors to this book. The task of compiling it has been equivalent to a holiday in itself and a reminder that, with or without steam, Iberia will be pleasant and welcoming as ever.

M.J.F.

2-8-2+2-8-2 Garratt 282-0421 climbing up from Fuente la Higuera towards La Encina with a freight train which includes the Valencia breakdown crane. Similar to the 1930 Central Aragon engines, these RENFE additions were built by Babcock and Wilcox in 1960./*M.J.F.*

CP(SS) Henschel 4-cylinder compound Pacific on a goods train at Setubal. Some were ultimately transferred to the Minho-Douro section but 552 stayed on its home ground. */W. J. V Anderson*

Introduction

The *Red Nacional de los Ferrocarriles Españoles*, or Spanish National Railway Network, was created in 1943 as an amalgamation of all the public railways using the Spanish standard gauge of 1674mm. Its major constituents were the *Norte*, MZA (*Madrid, Zaragoza y Alicante*), the *Andaluces* and the *Oeste*. As their names imply, these companies had been concerned respectively with lines in the Northern, Eastern, Southern and Western sectors of the country, but by the time of nationalisation this was no more guide to their extent, or the ownership of particular lines, than was the case with the four British companies.

The pictures presented on the following pages span approximately the last 15 years of RENFE steam. This begins in a period when there was limited electrification of Spanish railway lines and little diesel motive power. At that time there were a number of locomotives in service which had reached or were approaching their hundredth birthday, and engines 80 or more years old were commonplace. In contrast *La Maquinista Terrestre y Maritima* had turned out RENFE's last steam express engines in 1955-56, these being the imposing 4-8-4s, and in 1960-61 the *Sociedad Española de Construcciones Babcock & Wilcox* delivered a batch of 2-8-2+2-8-2 Garratts.

The mid-1960s saw a rapid modernisation of the RENFE, which included the swift disappearance of all the older locomotives and then of all others except the larger locomotives of standard two-cylinder classes. At the time of writing only a few standard 2-8-2s remain, of a large class built variously by the North British Locomotive Company of Glasgow and by the four major Spanish constructors; MTM at Barcelona, Babcock & Wilcox and Euskalduna both of Bilbao, and Macosa (formerly Devis) at Valencia.

The details of the manufacturers of the RENFE locomotives, representing builders all over Europe and the USA, and of the changes in ownership which took place before formation of RENFE are a fascinating study outside the scope of this book. Interested readers are recommended to refer to *Steam on the RENFE* by L. G. Marshall for this information.

The *Companhia dos Caminhos de Ferro Portugueses* is the Portuguese counterpart of RENFE, and was formed in 1947, the situation in Portugal differing in that narrow-gauge lines were also included in the merger.

The Portuguese broad gauge is the same as in Spain, and the principal companies involved in the formation of the CP were the original CP, representing the majority of lines between Lisbon and Oporto, and two groups of state-owned lines. These were the *Sul e Soeste* (CPss), providing communications in the south and south-east of the country and the *Minho-Douro* section (CPMD), serving the areas north of Oporto. Also noteworthy are the *Beira-Alta* company with the distinctive locomotives built for its hilly Pampilhosa-Guarda route, and the electrified Estoril line providing a suburban service to Lisbon, which was excluded from the merger. Prior to their amalgamation there was already close collaboration between the CP, CPss and CPMD and the pictures of the engines provided for them show strong family resemblances.

The narrow-gauge lines were all built to metre-gauge and were previously owned by various companies. Some of the feeder lines to the broad gauge were owned by the CPMD, whilst others belonged to the *Companhia Nacional*, the *Norte de Portugal*, or the *Valle do Vouga*.

The Portuguese pictures selected for this book again cover a span of 15 years. When this period opened electrification of the Lisbon-Oporto main line had already commenced, and a number of main-line diesel locomotives and multiple-units had been purchased in addition. The steam locomotives which were still operating included neither such old ones as in Spain (none built earlier than 1875), nor so many modern ones; most dated from the first quarter of the century. However, the transition from steam to other forms of motive power has progressed more gradually than in Spain with the result that Portuguese broad-gauge steam outlasted that of Spain, and the Corgo narrow-gauge line is still 100 per cent steam-worked as this book is published.

Portuguese locomotive stock is not as well documented as its Spanish counterpart, but a chapter on the narrow gauge figures in *Steam on the Sierra* by P. C. Allen and R. A. Wheeler. Stock lists have appeared in *The Railways of Portugal* by C. P. Boocock and A. Trickett in *Railway World* for August and September 1963, and also in *Railway Holiday in Portugal* by D. W. Winkworth.

The Minor Railways section of the book portrays the Spanish narrow-gauge public railways, as well as industrial railways and locomotives of all gauges. Since the very few Portuguese industrial locomotives are not depicted, the representatives in this category too are wholly Spanish.

The narrow-gauge railways of Spain were fascinating in their variety of gauge and appearance; the survivors are still attractive, albeit steamless. The commonest sub-standard gauge was one metre, but there were many others, mostly narrower, whilst one line which features in this section was built to the European standard gauge of 1435mm or 4ft 8½in, for which reason the Spanish 1674mm gauge will be referred to as 'broad'.

Having remarked on the rapid disappearance of steam on RENFE during the 1960s I have to echo the observation in respect of the narrow gauge, except that the change was often not to a different form of motive power but closure, for road transport has become increasingly competitive. Even so, the chain of metre-gauge lines along the north coast has been completed by the opening of the Ferrol-Gijon line.

What steam operation remains is all in an industrial context; the *FC Ponferrada-Villablino*, which provides the last steam-hauled narrow-gauge passenger service, and is indeed wholly steam-worked, is primarily a coal-hauling line, owned by *Minero Siderurgica de Ponferrada*. The Andorra-Escatron railway, opened in 1953 and worked by broad-gauge 4-8-4T locomotives including *Maquinista's* last steam order, is an adjunct of *Empresa Nacional de Electricidad S.A.* (ENDESA); and the broad-gauge steam engines working at the collieries and steelworks around Oviedo, including several RENFE refugees, belong to HUNOSA (*Hulleras del Norte S.A.*) or to ENSIDESA (*Empresa Nacional Siderurgica S.A.*).

The stock of the Spanish industrial operations is listed in the Industrial Railway Society's pocketbook SP, *Industrial Locomotives and Railways of Spain and Portugal*, and descriptions and stock lists of the public narrow-gauge lines are the subject of *Steam on the Sierra* by P. C. Allen and R. A. Wheeler.

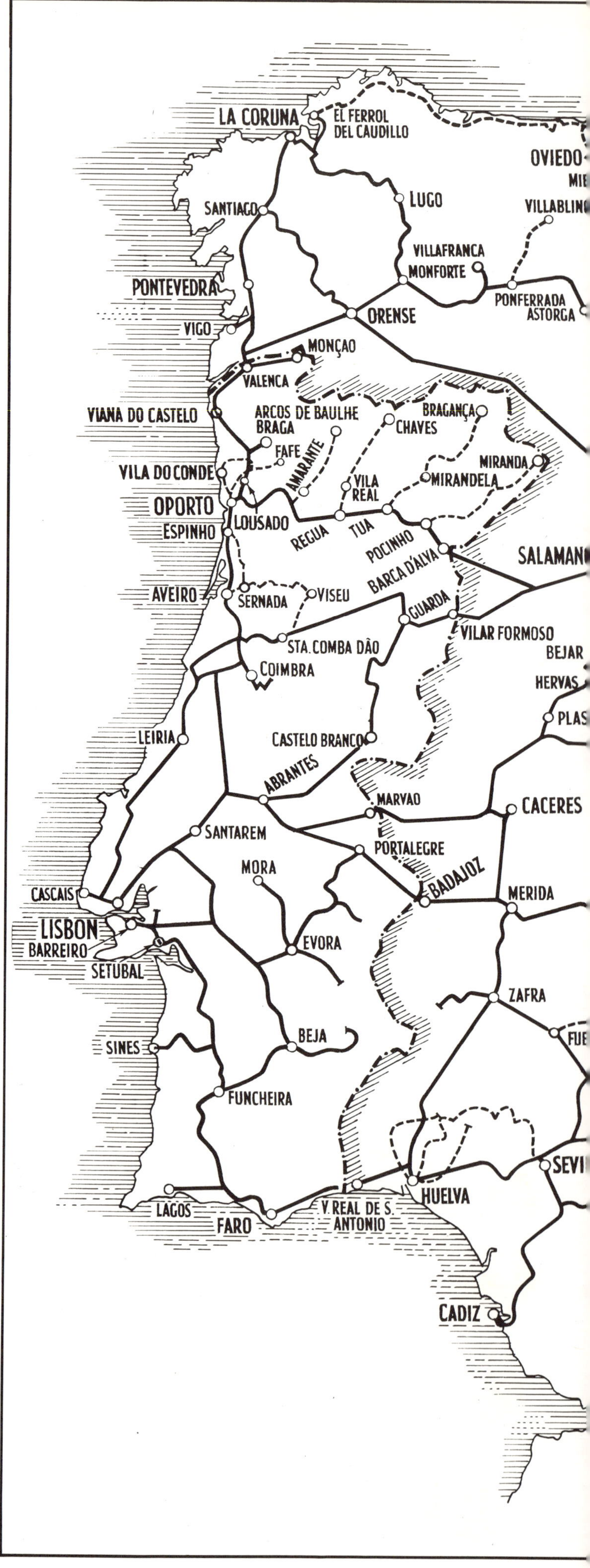

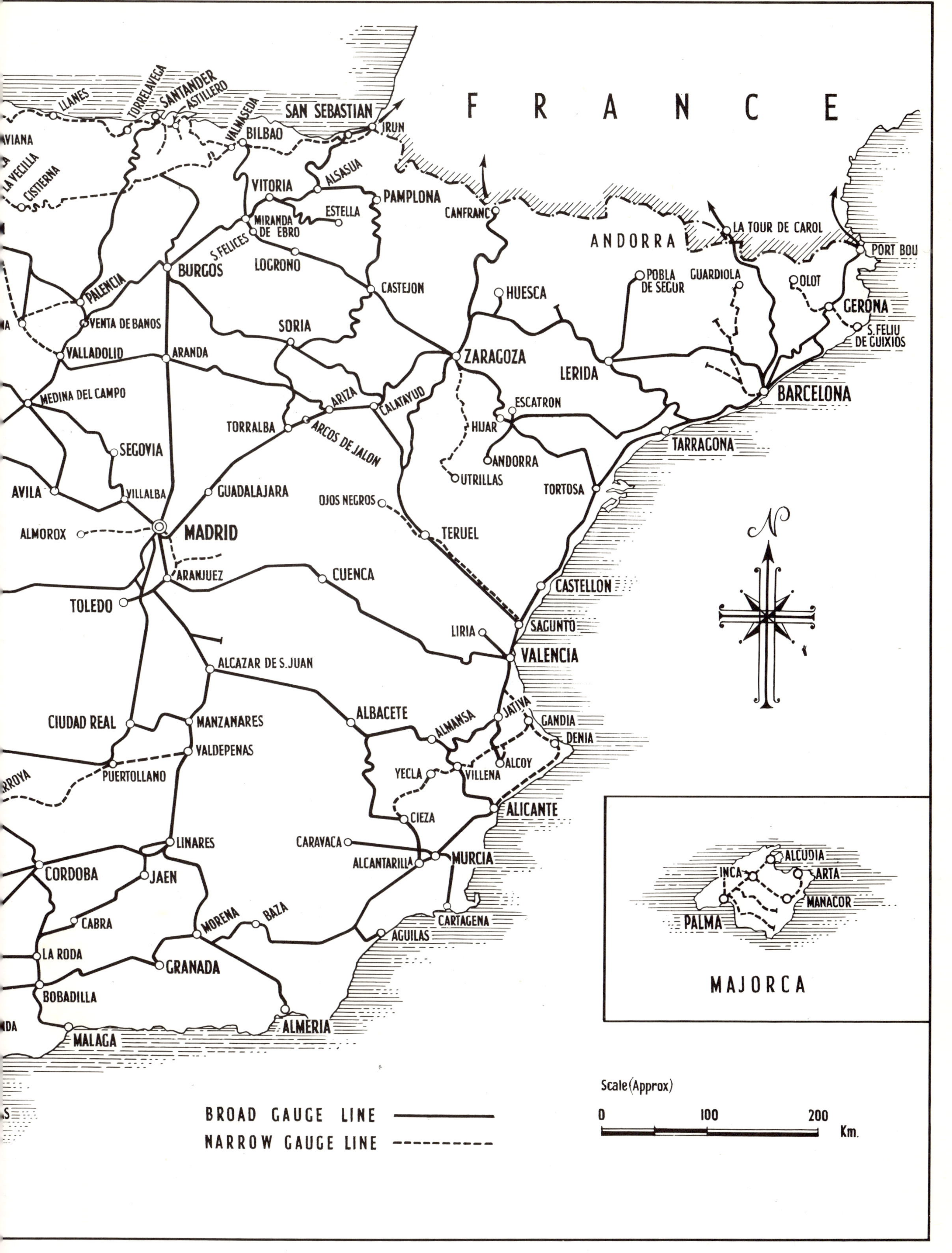

FRANCE
ANDORRA
SAN SEBASTIAN
IRUN
SANTANDER
TORRELAVEGA
ASTILLERO
LLANES
VALMASEDA
BILBAO
VITORIA
ALSASUA
PAMPLONA
ESTELLA
MIRANDA DE EBRO
S. FELICES
LOGRONO
BURGOS
PALENCIA
VENTA DE BANOS
VALLADOLID
ARANDA
SORIA
CASTEJON
CANFRANC
HUESCA
ZARAGOZA
LA TOUR DE CAROL
PORT BOU
POBLA DE SEGUR
GUARDIOLA
OLOT
GERONA
S. FELIU DE GUIXIOS
LERIDA
BARCELONA
TARRAGONA
TORTOSA
ESCATRON
HIJAR
ANDORRA
UTRILLAS
CALATAYUD
ARIZA
ARCOS DE JALON
TORRALBA
MEDINA DEL CAMPO
SEGOVIA
AVILA
VILLALBA
GUADALAJARA
MADRID
ALMOROX
OJOS NEGROS
TERUEL
ARANJUEZ
CUENCA
TOLEDO
CASTELLON
SAGUNTO
LIRIA
VALENCIA
ALCAZAR DE S. JUAN
CIUDAD REAL
MANZANARES
VALDEPENAS
PUERTOLLANO
ALBACETE
ALMANSA
JATIVA
GANDIA
DENIA
ALCOY
YECLA
VILLENA
ALICANTE
CIEZA
CARAVACA
ALCANTARILLA
MURCIA
CARTAGENA
AGUILAS
LINARES
CORDOBA
JAEN
CABRA
MORENA
BAZA
LA RODA
GRANADA
BOBADILLA
ALMERIA
MALAGA
VIANA
LA VECILLA
CISTIERNA
ALCUDIA
INCA
ARTA
MANACOR
PALMA
MAJORCA
Scale (Approx)
0
100
200
Km.
BROAD GAUGE LINE
NARROW GAUGE LINE

RENFE

Left: One of the last lines in Spain to retain steam workings was the Pamplona loop. The Castejón-Alsasua *omnibus* is seen near Villanueva-Araquil behind standard 2-8-2s 141-2369 and 141-2231./*M.J.F.*

Bottom left: A *Norte* 4-cylinder compound 4-8-0, 240-4020, leaves San Felices on a Miranda-Zaragoza train./*M. Pope*

Below: Morning mist in the Ebro valley near San Felices./*M.J.F.*

Above: A *Norte* 2-8-0 leaving San Felices on a Logrono-Miranda freight./*M. Pope*

Top right: RENFE standard 2-8-2 141-2125 near San Felices on the 18.15 Miranda-Casetas stopping train. This engine is one of the original batch built by North British Loco Co in 1952; subsequent additions were supplied by Spanish builders./*B. Stephenson*

Right: Massive power for a three-coach local near San Felices; a standard 4-8-2 and 2-8-2 bound for Miranda./*W. J. V. Anderson*

Above: Once a familiar sight at Miranda de Ebro, a RENFE 4-8-4 backs on to a Madrid express./*M. Dunnett*

Top right: The up 'Iberia Express' leaving Miranda de Ebro in steam days, with RENFE compound 4-8-2 241-4075 piloting 4-8-4 242-2007./*W. H. C. Kelland, courtesy Bournemouth Railway Club*

Right: A standard 2-8-2 crossing the Rio Ebro at Miranda with a southbound freight train. /*B. Stephenson*

Top left: A standard 4-8-4 at the head of a Madrid-bound express in the pass of Pancorbo./*P. W. Gray*

Left: RENFE 2-8-2s 141-2269 and 141-2391 storming up-grade near Bujedo with an up freight. The date is May 1968 and electrification works on this section are already complete./*B. Stephenson*

Above: Standard 2-8-2 141-2223 piloting ex-MZA semi-streamlined 4-8-2 241-2109 away from a check at Pancorbo, also in May 1968./*B. Stephenson*

Below: An MZA 4-8-2 tackles the climb to Pancorbo with an Irun-Madrid train, October 1966./*M.J.F.*

Right: A 4-8-4 storms out of the mountain pass at Pancorbo with a Bilbao-Madrid express./*M.J.F.*

Bottom right: MZA 'bathtub' 4-8-2 pulls away from Pancorbo with an up passenger train./*M.J.F.*

Left: A pair of 4-8-2s, MZA and standard, leave Pancorbo with the afternoon stopping train to Madrid./*M. Dunnett*

Above: The northbound 'Iberia Express' leaving Burgos behind a pair of RENFE 4-8-4s./*I. S. Krause*

Right: Norte 4-8-2 241-4037 seen at Palencia on the combined Reinosa and Leon to Valladolid *omnibus.* 4-8-0 240-4043, another *Norte* compound, had brought in the Leon portion./*P. W. Gray*

Top right: Norte 2-8-0 140-2349 on the turntable at Vigo, overlooked by an *Oeste* 4-8-0./*P. Ransome-Wallis*

Right: The one-time Vigo shed pilot, 0-6-0ST 030-0201 *Sar,* was built by Hunslet in 1880 for the *West Galicia* railway. /*P. Ransome-Wallis*

Below: An ex-*Norte* ALCO 2-8-2 141-2014 passes *Norte* 2-8-0 140-2312 at Vigo. /*P. Ransome-Wallis*

Right: Shrinking-on a driving-wheel tyre at Vigo depot./*P. Ransome-Wallis*

Below: Oeste (originally *Medina del Campo-Zamora-Orense-Vigo*) 4-8-0 240-2054 waiting to leave La Coruña on a Vigo train. /*J. E. Bell*

Above: A 1963 scene at Avila, with standard locomotives 141-2296 and 240-2494 arriving on a freight from the north, and passing 0-8-0 040-2002 built in 1865./*P. W. Gray*

Below: MZA 4-8-4T 242-0278 passing 'light engine' through Medina del Campo station. /*V. Hand*

Top right: Ex-MZA 4-8-2 241-2082 waiting for its next duty at Salamanca depot, one night in May 1968./*V. Hand*

Bottom right: Contrasting expressions on three faces at Salamanca; MZA 4-8-4T 242-0278, *Norte* 2-8-0 140-2212, and the Crosti rebuild from the same class, 140-2438./*P. Riley*

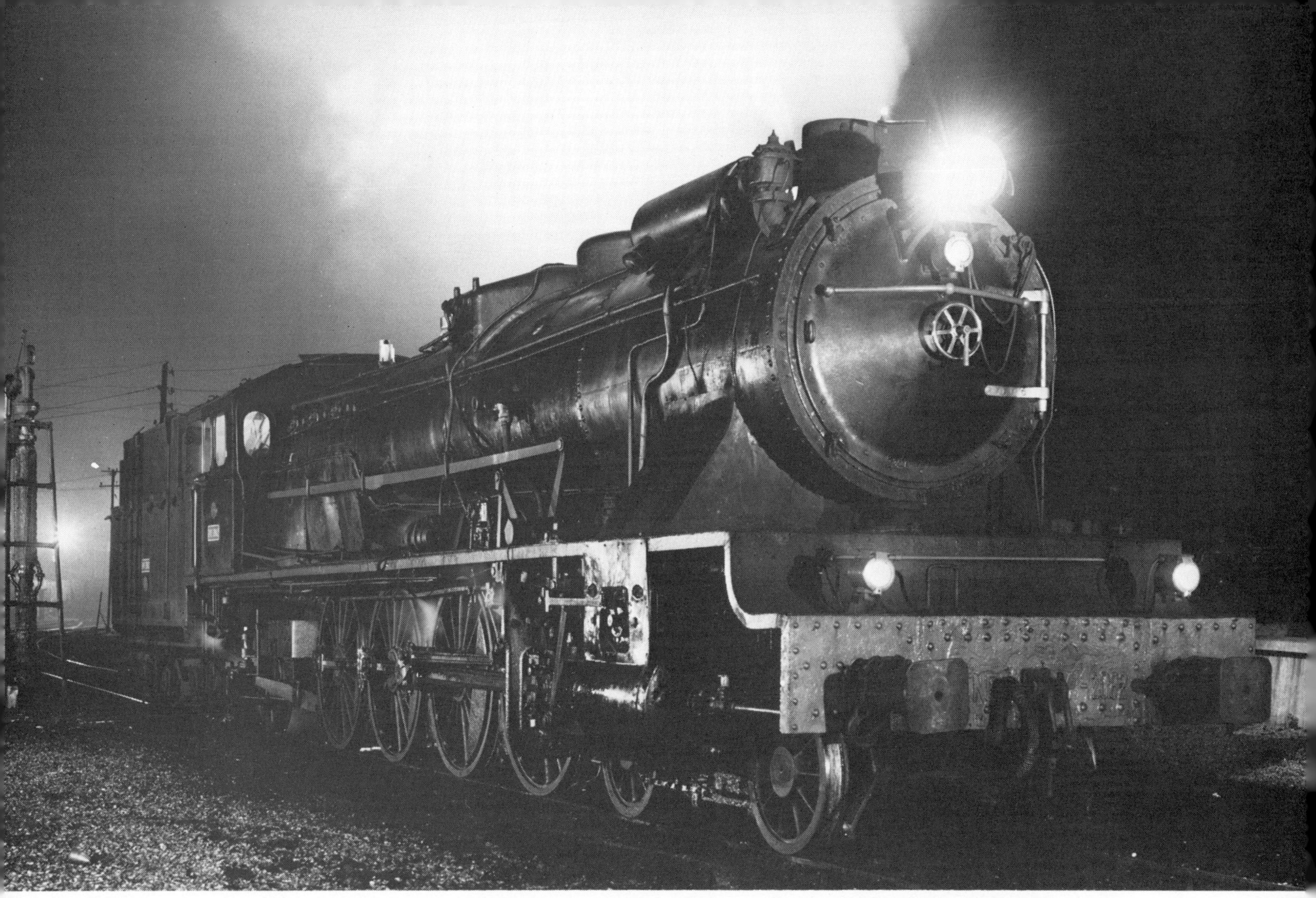

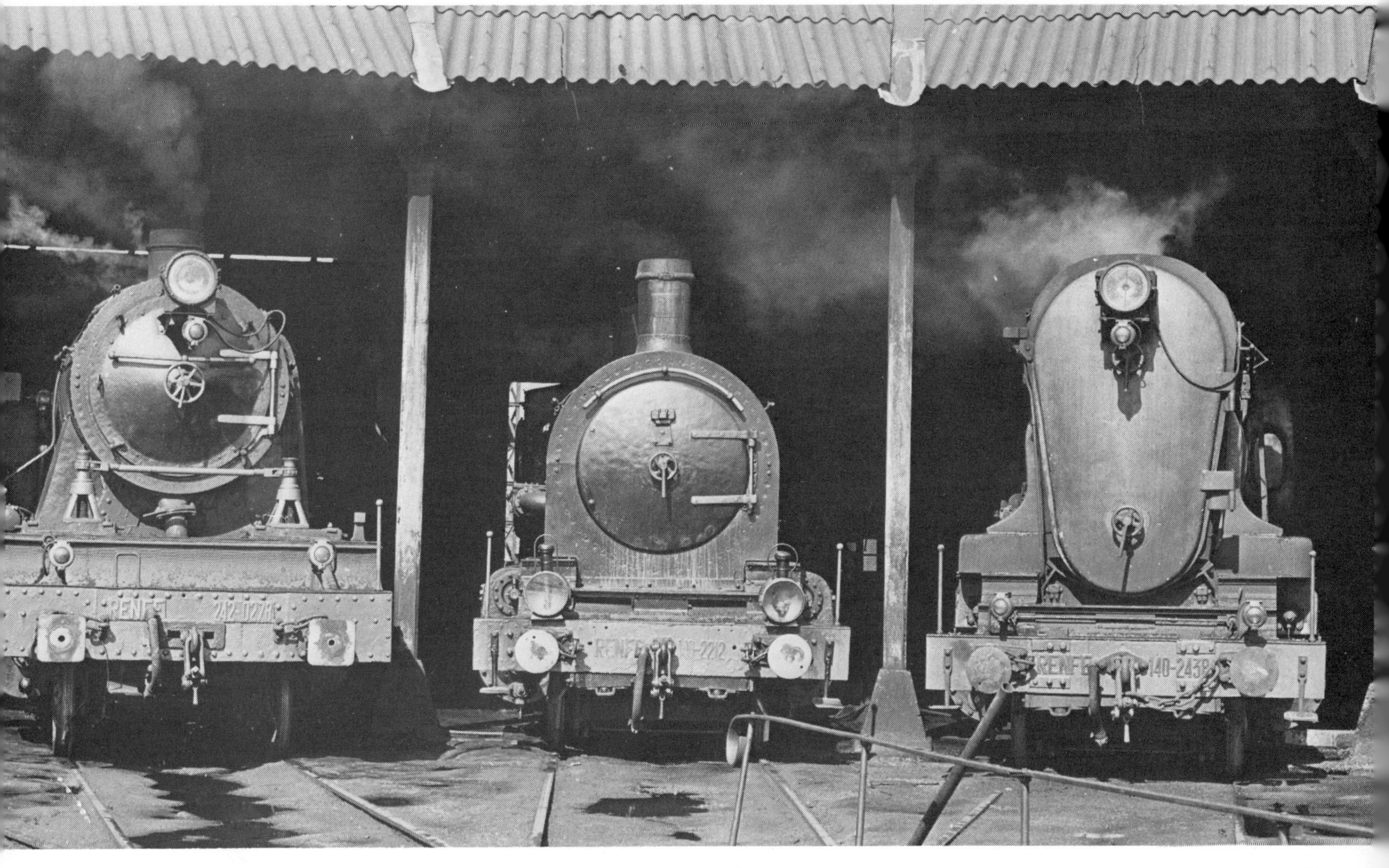
RENFE 242-0278
RENFE
RENFE 140-2438

Above: The Lisbon portion of the 'Iberia Express' between Salamanca and the Portuguese frontier behind an MZA 4-8-2. */V. Hand*

Left: Rebuilt MZA 4-8-2 241-2087 captured climbing away from Salamanca with the 14.25 to Astorga, May 1968./*B. Stephenson*

Right: MZA 4-8-0 240-2287 near Bejar on an Arroyo-Salamanca freight./*V. Hand*

Below: A Salamanca station scene showing Hartmann 0-6-0 030-2531 built in 1901 for the MCP, and *Oeste* 4-8-0 240-2238. */L. G. Marshall*

Below: Late March snow at Hervas, and an MZA 4-8-0 restarting a Palazuelo-Salamanca freight./*J. R. P. Hunt*

Right: The roundhouse of Delicias depot, Madrid, showing *Oeste* 4-6-0 230-2065, MZA 'bathtub' 4-8-2 241-2106 and MZA 0-6-0 030-2117, which was built in 1861. /*P. W. Gray*

Bottom right: Oeste (MCP) Mogul 130-2114 shunting Madrid Delicias goods yard. /*L. G. Marshall*

RENFE
230-2065

Left: Standard 2-8-2 141-2335 leaving the passenger terminus at Delicias./*V. Hand*

Bottom left: One-time *Madrid-Cacares-Portugal* 4-6-0 230-2065 waiting to leave Delicias with a stopping train for Talavera, March 1966./*L. G. Marshall*

Below: The MZA terminus at Atocha, Madrid, with a standard 2-8-2 arriving, and 4-8-2 waiting to leave./*P. W. Gray*

Bottom: A platform-end pastorale at Aranda de Duero, 1967. Outside the shed are the Crosti-boilered 2-8-0 and an *Oeste* 4-8-0. By this time the latter class had been transferred from Vigo to work the Valladolid-Ariza line. /*I. S. Krause*

Left: RENFE 3-cylinder 2-10-2 151-3102 storming up towards Torralba with a short freight train from Arcos de Jalón. Originally built for the Ponferrada coal traffic, the type finished its life on the Zaragoza-Madrid line./*M.J.F.*

Bottom left: Former *Santander-Mediterraneo* 2-8-0 140-2516 near Soria on a Burgos-Calatayud train. This railway was only opened in 1928 and the Babcock & Wilcox 2-8-0s remained on it throughout their lives./*M.J.F.*

Below: A *Norte* 4-6-0 approaching Soria on the Torralba-Soria line./*M.J.F.*

RENFE

Top left: Norte 2-8-0 140-2100 shunting the hump yard at Zaragoza (Arrabal) whilst sisters 140-2209 and 140-2254 arrive on a goods train./*P. W. Gray*

Bottom left: Two MZA 4-cylinder compounds head a troop train through Zaragoza — 4-6-0 230-4051 piloting 4-8-0 240-4069. /*P. Ransome-Wallis*

Above: In 1960 the shed pilot at Zaragoza, (Campo Sepulcro) was a tenderless 0-6-0, built by Kitson in 1858./*M.J.F.*

Below: Arrabal was the *Norte* depot in Zaragoza, and here a group of *Norte* 0-8-0s are seen grouped round one of the turntables in 1960./*M.J.F.*

Above: An MZA 4-6-4T, built in 1903 by Maffei, 232-0205 was working the Lérida depot staff train in September 1969./*E. J. Dew*

Below: A 2-8-2 + 2-8-2 Garratt crossing the Rio Segre at Lérida, bound for Tarragona. /*I. K. Samson*

Right: An ex-MZA 4-8-0 crossing the viaduct at Villanueva on the Lérida to Pobla de Segur branch./*J. R. P. Hunt*

Above: A RENFE 4-8-2, passes through Tamarite-Altorricón with a Barcelona-Zaragoza express, whilst an MZA 4-8-0 waits for the road./*W. J. V. Anderson*

Below: A standard 2-8-2 near Ager on the Pobla de Segur branch./*J. R. P. Hunt*

Right: A *Central Aragon* 2-8-2 + 2-8-2 Garratt at La Riba with a Tarragona-Lérida freight. /*W. J. V. Anderson*

Left: Norte 0-6-0 030-0204 *Tarraco,* seen at Tarragona, was built by Schneider in 1864. */P. Ransome-Wallis*

Below: *Central Aragon* 4-6-2 + 2-6-4 Garratt on a Barcelona-Valencia train in the outskirts of Tarragona.*/P. Ransome-Wallis*

Right: Contrasting motive power at Tarragona. The 0-8-0 is 040-2012 built for the *Tarragona-Barcelona-Francia* railway by Sharp Stewart in 1878.*/P. Ransome-Wallis*

Below right: A typical RENFE lamp on *Tarraco.*/*P. W. Gray*

Top left: A Barcelona-Valencia train, with MZA 4-8-0 piloting a CA Pacific Garratt, intercepted near Hospitalet./*P. Ransome-Wallis*

Bottom left: An MZA 4-8-2 rebuilt with Lentz valve gear, 241-2091 was seen on a Barcelona-Murcia train near Cambrils. /*P. Ransome-Wallis*

Above: 040-2534, an ex-*Norte* Henschel 0-8-0, was yard pilot at Tortosa in September 1967./*J. R. P. Hunt*

Below: Central Aragon 0-6-0 030-2472 was photographed working a Valencia-Caudiel train near Sagunto./*P. Ransome-Wallis*

Above: Ex-*Norte* 0-6-0 030-2077 *La Cañada,* leaving Valencia Termino on the Villamarchante *correo./P. Ransome-Wallis*

Below: Norte 4-6-0 230-2013, built in 1904 by Hanomag, leaving Valencia on a stopping train which included double-deck coaches. */D. Trevor Rowe*

Top right: A detail of *Central Aragon* double-Pacific Garratt 462-0401, built by Euskalduna in 1930./*R. K. Evans*

Bottom right: A delightful 0-6-0, seen on Valencia Termino depot in 1960; 030-2368 was originally No 3 of the *FC Alcantarilla-Lorca,* supplied by Sharp Stewart in 1884./*M.J.F.*

Top left: Norte 4-6-0s of two different series, 230-2075 and 230-2021, double-head the Madrid *correo* out of Valencia, March 1965. */L. G. Marshall*

Left: Norte 0-6-0 030-2086 (Hartmann, 1882) arriving at Valencia Termino on the 17.46 from Villamarchante, May 1963. */P. W. Gray*

Above: Norte 4-6-0 230-2091 entering Jativa on a freight from Valencia.*/P. Riley*

Left: Central Aragon passenger Garratt 462-0406 near Fuente La Higuera with a Valencia-Madrid oil train./*J. R. P. Hunt*

Right: A view from under the water tower at Fuente La Higuera as a freight for La Encina pulls out of the loop./*M. Dunnett*

Below: Central Aragon 0-6-6-0 Mallet 060-4008 climbing towards Venta Mina on the direct Valencia-Madrid line with a freight train for Cuenca./*P. Riley*

Top left: MZA 4-8-0 240-2246 approaching Almansa on the double-track section from La Encina./*M.J.F.*

Left: MZA 4-8-0 240-2265 roaring away from La Encina with a freight for Valencia. /*W. J. V. Anderson*

Above: Former *Norte* 0-6-0 030-2072 put out to grass behind the shed at Albacete. /*M. Dunnett*

PEPITA
MANOLITA

Top left: A standard 4-8-0 heading out of Alicante towards La Encina./*M. Dunnett*

Left: Central Aragon 0-6-6-0 Mallet 060-4007, at the end of its days, taking a Murcia train through the suburbs of Alicante in 1966./*M.J.F.*

Above: Algeciras-Bobadilla 4-4-0 220-2021, built by Beyer Peacock in 1891, on shed at Alicante in 1960./*M.J.F.*

Right: Originally built for the *Medina del Campo-Salamanca* railway, 2-6-0 130-2083 leaving Alicante for Cartagena./*M. Dunnett*

Top left: Two of the *Oeste* Henschel 2-6-0s, 130-2082 and 130-2083 cross at Beniajan on the Murcia-Alicante line./*L. G. Marshall*

Bottom left: Two of the *Great Southern* 2-6-0s head a goods train out of Alcantarilla towards their home line. The leading engine is 130-2139 *Olula,* built by Sharp Stewart in 1901./*W. J. V. Anderson*

Above: Andaluces 2-8-0 140-2055 climbing away from Guadix on the 13.50 to Baza, May 1966./*P. W. Gray*

Below: 140-2063 of the same class built by Babcock & Wilcox in 1928, near Benelua de Guadix on the Granada-Alicante *correo.* /*P. W. Gray*

Above: The view from a Granada-Guadix train approaching Iznalloz./*D. Trevor Rowe*

Below: Ex-*Oeste* 2-8-2T 141-0217 approaching Granada on a mixed train from Moreda. Two similar engines were supplied to the Baza-Guadix railway and in due course RENFE transferred the *Oeste* engines to the Guadix-Granada area./*L. G. Marshall*

Top right: 240-2018 and 240-2036, representing the earliest class of *Andaluces* 4-8-0, leave Granada on the Seville *correo.* /*L. G. Marshall*

Bottom right: Built by Baldwin in 1920, *Andaluces* 2-8-0 140-2007 approaches Granada from the Bobadilla line, banked by an *Oeste* 2-8-2T./*L. G. Marshall*

Top left: Andaluces 4-8-0 240-2047 (Hanomag 1922) leaving Salinas on the 10.15 Granada-Bobadilla, May 1966./*P. W. Gray*

Bottom left: Two old 0-6-0s at Malaga; *Andaluces* 030-2495 on empty stock, and MZA 030-2352 on a rubbish train. /*P. Ransome-Wallis*

Above: Andaluces 0-6-0 030-2542 at Algeciras harbour./*L. G. Marshall*

Below: Three 4-8-0s on Ronda shed were (from left) 240-2516 of an *Andaluces* design which became a RENFE standard, and 240-2441, 240-2438 both earlier *Andaluces* engines./*L. G. Marshall*

Top left: This diminutive 0-4-0WT, originally supplied by Schneider in 1871 to the *F C Urbano de Jerez,* ended its life on the untaxing duties of the Seville staff train./*L. G. Marshall*

Bottom left: Ex-MZA 0-6-0 030-2362 passing through Seville (San Bernardo) station on empty stock, August 1966./*W. G. Sumner*

Above: MZA Alco Pacific 231-2011 entering Utrera on a Seville-Granada *correo.* /*L. G. Marshall*

Below: Andaluces 2-6-0 130-2036 leaving Cabra on the daily Puente Genil-Linares *correo.* These engines were rebuilt at Malaga from a class of earlier mixed-traffic 0-6-0s. /*L. G. Marshall*

Above: Andaluces 2-8-0 140-2022 leaving Lucena for Puente Genil. They were derived in similar fashion to the 2-6-0s, in this case from a group of St Leonard 0-8-0s./*P. W. Gray*

Below: Andaluces 2-6-0s 130-2053 and 130-2036 climbing up to Jaen on a train from Linares./*P. W. Gray*

Top right: Andaluces 4-8-0 240-2026 passing MZA 0-8-0 040-2273 whilst leaving Cercadilla on a Cordoba-Almorchon freight. /*L. G. Marshall*

Right: Andaluces 4-8-0s 240-2037 and 240-2049 on the long slog up from Cordoba with the 06.00 to Almorchon./*P. W. Gray*

CP
C.P.
294

Left: CP 4-6-0 294, built by Henschel & Sohn of Kassel in 1913, seen on the Monçâo-Viana mixed train near Carreço in 1971./*M.J.F.*

Above: Henschel compound 4-6-0 354 preparing to leave Barreiro with a Beja train in 1964./*P. W. Gray*

Below: The station pilot at Barreiro in 1959, Hannoversche 0-6-0 46, built 1886./*L. King*

Left: In 1945 the Portuguese heavy motive power was strengthened by the delivery of a number of 2-8-2s from Alco. 871 was on shed at Barreiro in 1965./*R. K. Evans*

Below: Pacific 555 heads an express out of Barreiro, bound for Funcheira in September 1959./*A. Trickett*

Top right: CP 4-8-0 831 poses outside Barreiro shed. Built in 1947 by La Maquinista at Barcelona, it was part of an order of six engines shared between three Spanish builders./*A. Trickett*

Right: With the onset of electrification, steam traction in Lisbon itself disappeared more quickly than at Barreiro across the river. 025 was a Beyer Peacock 0-6-2T of 1890, photographed at Santa Apollonia depot in 1959./*A. Trickett*

Bottom right: SACM 0-8-0 613, built in 1890, shunting the marshalling yard at Entroncamento./*A. Trickett*

Top left: Two of the CP's celebrated *'mouse'* class, shed pilots at Entroncamento: 001 built by Richard Hartmann at Chemnitz in 1881, and 004 by the Belgian firm of John Cockerill./*P. W. Gray*

Bottom left: Massive Henschel 2-8-4T 0224 pulls out of Entroncamento yard, past the back of the roundhouse./*P. Ransome-Wallis*

Above: Coimbra — B, junction for the city of Coimbra, with Fives 4-6-0 compound 270 on a Porto-Coimbra train, and 2-8-4T 0217. /*P. Ransome-Wallis*

Below: Two four-cylinder compounds at Pampilhosa depot; Borsig 4-6-0 242 and Henschel 4-8-0 803, culmination of the Beira-Alta compounds./*P. Ransome-Wallis*

C.P.
103

Left: Esslingen 2-6-0T E103 climbing through the pinewoods near Torredeita on the metre-gauge Dão line./*W. J. V. Anderson*

Right: Borsig 4-6-0T 124 on a Viseu-Santa Comba Dão train gets 'all clear' from the crossing keeper at a typical narrow-gauge level crossing./*M.J.F.*

Below: Norte de Portugal 2-4-6-0T compound Mallet E182 near Bodiosa on a Sernada-Viseu train./*W. J. V. Anderson*

C.P.
E121

CARVALHAL
PORTELA
C.P.
E94

Left: Borsig 4-6-0T 121 heads a light Sernada-Viseu local near Ribeiradio./*L. A. Nixon*

Below left: Decauville 2-6-0T E94 on the Aveiro line at Carvalhal da Portela. /*I. K. Samson*

Right: Valle do Vouga 2-8-2T E131 accelerating away from Sernada with the morning mixed train to Espinho./*M.J.F.*

Below: Norte de Portugal 0-4-4-0T compound Mallet E151 at Eixo on the Aviero line. /*W. J. V. Anderson*

Left: Esslingen 2-6-0T E84, built in 1886 crossing the Rio Vouga at Sernada, bound for Aviero. The Aveiro-Viseu section is now closed, and the bridge converted for road traffic./*W. J. V. Anderson*

Above: Decauville 2-6-0T E95 waiting to leave Sernada with an evening departure for Aveiro./*C. M. Whitehouse*

Below: 2-8-2T E133 on an Espinho-Oliveira mixed train at Coute de Cucujães./*S. C. Crook*

Above: Alco 2-8-2 870 setting out from Vila Nova de Gaia with a southbound freight on the Porto-Lisbon main line./*P. W. Gray*

Below: A 2-6-4T and southbound stopping train from Porto cross the river Douro. /*D. Simmonds*

Top right: For a time during the 1960s the CP hired some *Norte* 2-8-0s from the RENFE. Here one is seen working over Eiffel's Dona Maria Pia bridge, which spans the Douro between Campanha and Gaia. At left is the steep incline from Alfandega goods yard to Campanha./*W. J. V. Anderson*

Bottom right: Beyer-Peacock 0-6-2T 014 shunting the Alfandega goods yard in Porto. These MD engines were smaller-wheeled equivalents of the CP type illustrated earlier. /*L. King*

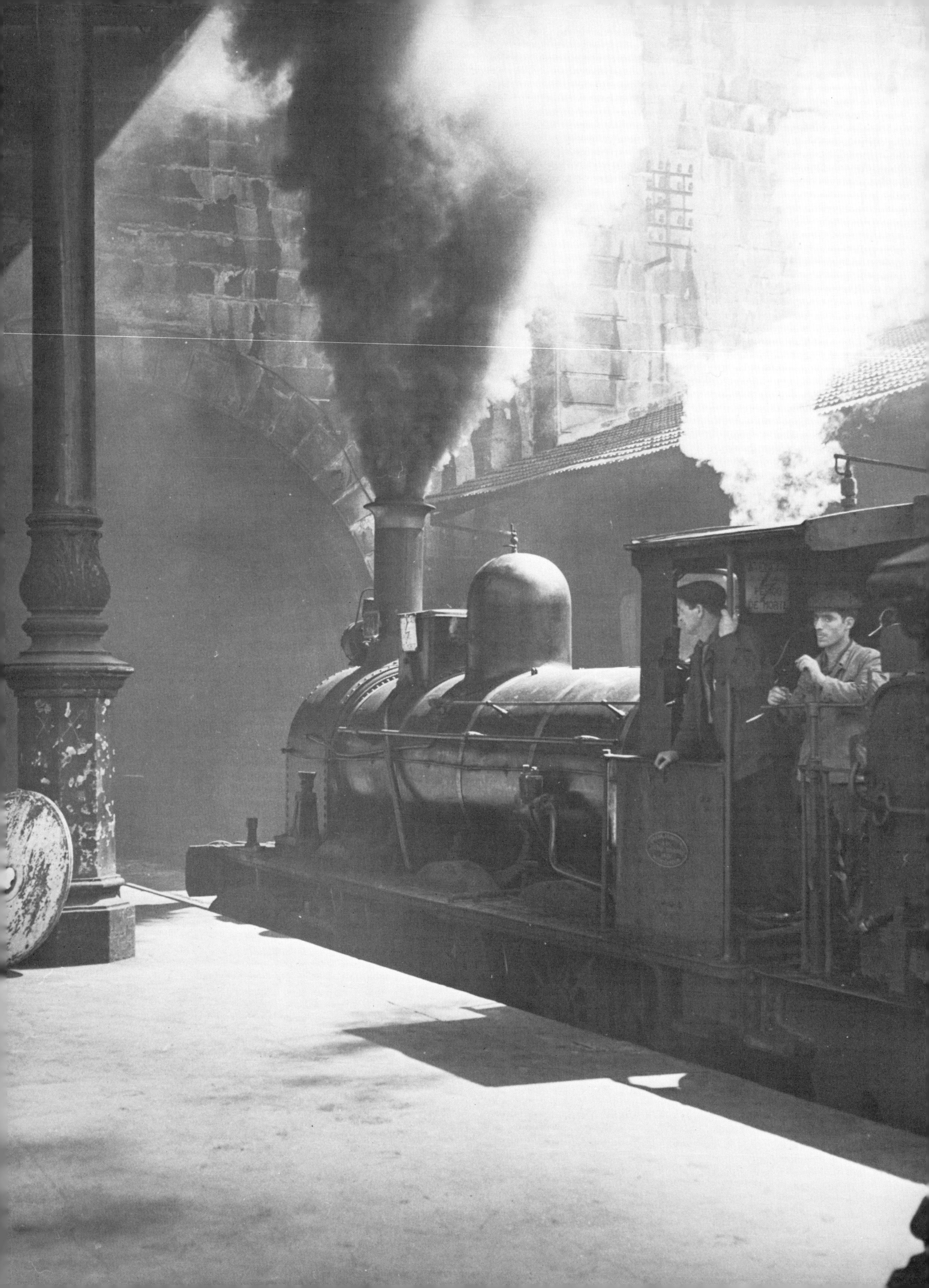

Above: Two ancient Beyer-Peacock engines at Campanha — 2-4-0 No 9 built in 1875 and 0-6-0 24./*P. W. Gray*

Left: Another delightful 1875 Beyer-Peacock 0-6-0, No 23, seen whilst station pilot at Porto's São Bento terminus./*D. J. Mitchell*

Below: Henschel inside-cylinder 4-6-0 285 climbing up from São Bento to Campanha whilst the electrification work was in progress./*W. J. V. Anderson*

Above: Ratinha 0-4-0WT 003 was a Cockerill engine of 1890, though the works plate was almost obliterated by polishing. This view is of the steam depot at Contumil, opened during the 1960s when Campanha was remodelled and the shed there closed./*M.J.F.*

Top right: A view of Contumil depot showing the Lisbon-assembled 2-6-4T 070 as well as Swiss and German-built examples of the same class./*W. J. V. Anderson*

Right: The last surviving 2-6-2T rebuild, No 033, seen shunting at Contumil yard. Originally a BP 1890 0-6-2T, its frames have been extended and a saddle-like water tank added beneath the new smokebox to give extra front weight./*R. W. Courtney*

POSTO
DE
MANUTENÇÃO
C.P. 087
C.P. 070
C.P. 295
033

Above: 2-6-4T 079 on Contumil shed with a pair of two-cylinder 2-8-0s. 705 and 713 both retained the copper chimney caps which most broad-gauge CP engines had already lost./*M.J.F.*

Below: NBL 4-cylinder compound 2-8-0 751 northbound between Contumil and Rio Tinto./*G. W. Morrison*

Right: Trindade, the metre-gauge terminus in Porto, handles a heavy commuter traffic from north of the city. Henschel 2-8-2T E141 of 1931 stands at the buffer-stops./*M. J. F.*

LINHA 3
C.P.
E141

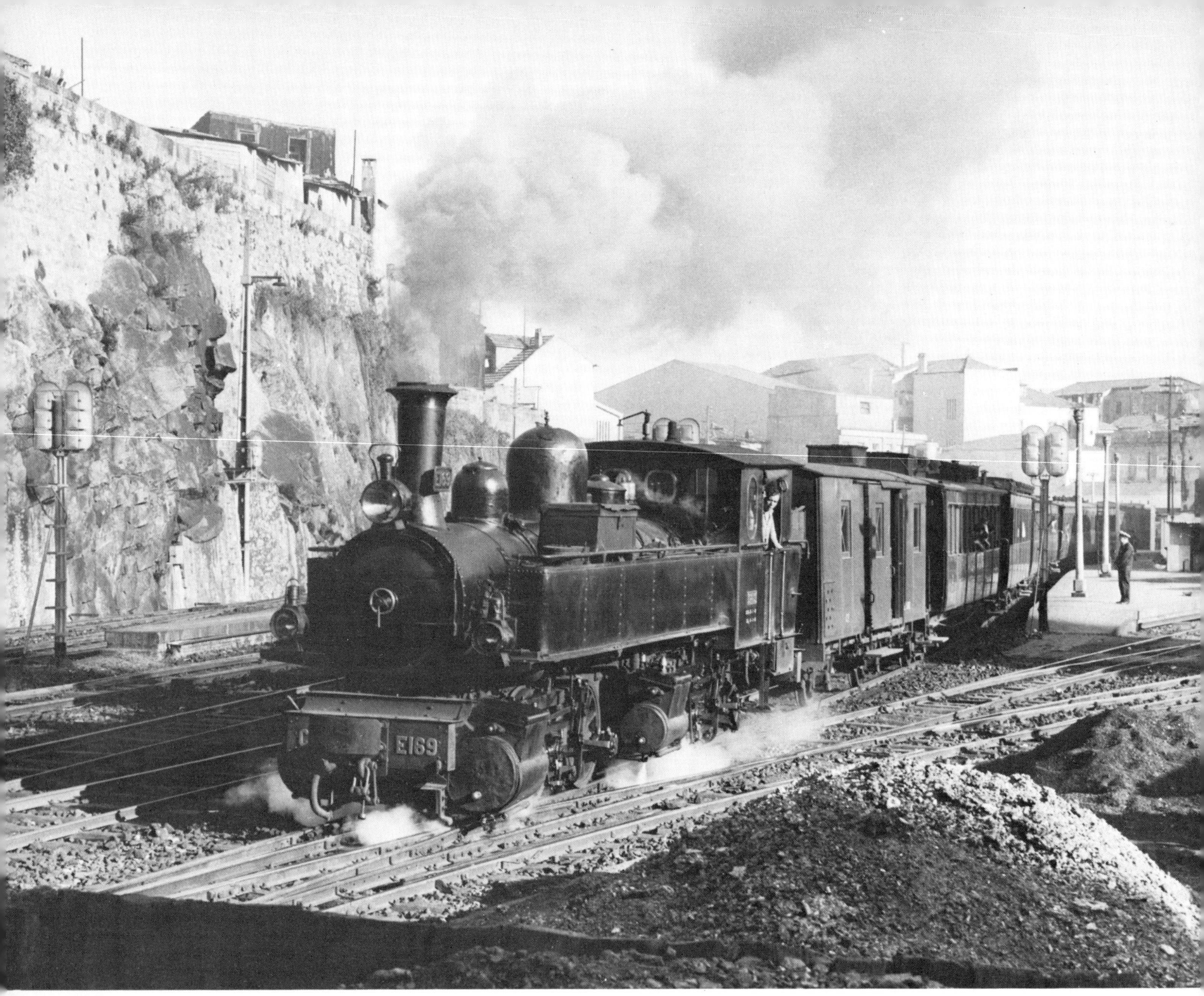

Above left: 0-4-4-0T Mallet E169 sets out from Trindade./*G. W. Murrison*

Left: The narrow-gauge depot at Boavista, seen from the platform at Avenida da França, with 2-6-0T E85 in the foreground./*M. J. F.*

Above: 2-8-2T E142 rolls into Avenida da França station, last stop before Trindade, with a train from Povoa de Varzim./*M.J.F.*

Right: 2-8-2T E141 waits at the junction of Senhora da Hora to set out on the double-track section into Porto./*C. M. Whitehouse*

Above: 0-4-4-0T Mallet E168 crossing the Rio Ave at Vila do Conde en route to Porto from Povoa./*G. W. Morrison*

Left: E141 coasts under the aqueduct north of Vila do Conde with a Povoa-Porto train./*M. J. F.*

Right: Mallet 0-4-4-0T E166 rolls away from Amorim with an early morning Povoa-Famalicão train./*M. J. F.*

C.P.
66

Left: 0-4-4-0T E166 nearing the summit of the Guimarães-Fafe section with a through train from Porto./*M. J. F.*

Below: Sparkling 0-4-4-0T E166 leaves the narrow-gauge end of Lousado station bound for Guimarães, passing Mallet E170 and 2-6-0T E102 on the shed./*W. J. V. Anderson*

Right: SLM-built 2-6-4T 074 on a Braga-Porto train near São Romão de Coronado. /*P. J. Robinson*

Below right: Trofa has broad and narrow gauge platforms. A 2-6-4T rolls in from Porto whilst 2-6-0T E85 waits to leave./*M. J. F.*

CP. 074

C.P. 236

C.P. 081

Left: Borsig 4-cylinder compound 4-6-0 236 sets off from Trofa bound for Porto, beside the narrow-gauge route to the same town. /*W. J. V. Anderson*

Below left: 2-6-4T 081 pulls out of the Braga branch platform at Nine with a stopping train from Porto./*G. W. Morrison*

Right: Pacific 560 being prepared for duty at Nine./*M. J. F.*

Below: Preserved 2-2-2ST CP(MD) 02049 drawn out of the shed at Braga by the branch 2-6-4T 086. This movement was for the benefit of an LCGB party visiting Portugal in 1959./*L. King*

Below: Henschel 2-8-4T 0188 leaving Viana do Castelo on an evening stopping train for Nine. These engines were a lighter version of the CP design, supplied for the Minho-Douro section./*M. J. F.*

Bottom: Henschel 4-6-0 293 near Carraço, on the evening Monção-Porto *correio*./*M.J.F.*

Right: Another view of the *correio* near Carraço, hauled by 560, one of the CP(SS) 4-6-2s after these had been drafted north of the Douro./*W. J. V. Anderson*

Below right: 2-8-4T 0187 exuberantly breasts a minor summit north of Afife at the head of the Monção-Viana mixed train./*M.J.F.*

C.P.

CP
501

Left: In contrast to the CP(SS) version, only one of the CP's Henschel Pacifics was drafted to Contumil. Last survivor 501 stands at Rede station on the 10.40 Barca d'Alva-Porto in April 1971, shortly before withdrawal after collision damage./*S. C. Crook*

Right: Schwartzkopff 4-cylinder 2-8-0 754 at Godim on the very slow 01.25 Porto-Regua mixed train./*S. C. Cook*

Below: 2-6-4T 070 near Godim on a Porto-Regua grape-pickers extra. Vintage time, 1968./*M. J. F.*

Left: Oily reflection at Regua of the maker's plate of Borsig 4-6-0 248./*J. R. P. Hunt*

Below: NBL 2-cylinder 2-8-0 719 arriving at Regua with the overnight mixed from Campanha./*J. S. Whiteley*

Right: A tantalising sight on a hot day at Regua./*J. R. P. Hunt*

Left: Metre-gauge Esslingen 0-6-0T E54 provokes discussion at Regua./*J. R. P. Hunt*

Below: One of the 'Portuguese B12s' (a nickname derived, of course, from their visual affinity with the B12 4-6-0s, of the LNER) much admired by British enthusiasts. Henschel inside-cylinder 4-6-0 282, built 1910, takes the evening train to Barca D'Alva on the Spanish border out of Regua. /*W. J. V. Anderson*

Right: Mallet 2-4-6-0T E202 being coaled at Regua./*C. M. Whitehouse*

Below right: Regua's narrow-gauge pilot, Henschel 0-4-0WT E1, shunts across a level crossing east of the station./*M. J. F.*

CP
E 202

FERREIRA
VILA SECA
GALAFURA

VILA POUCA DE AG
C.P.
209

C.P.
07

Left: One of the 2-4-6-0T Mallets has been fitted with a Giesl ejector. Here is E209 on a Corgo line train from Chaves to Regua at Vila Pouça de Aguiar./*W. J. V. Anderson*

Below left: 2-4-6-0T E207 setting out from Regua over mixed-gauge track./*M. J. F.*

Right: An inside-cylinder 4-6-0 draws the morning Regua-Poçinho mixed train out of São Mamede do Tua./*M. J. F.*

Below: Trailing a haze of smoke and alcohol, Alsacienne 0-6-0 CP 167 of 1889 leaves Tua on a returning port-promoting excursion with a party of Dutch importers. The engine had been recovered from the dump at Contumil and is seen cleaned, polished, and with decorations including the lid of a wine cask and the Dutch and Portuguese flags./*W. J. V. Anderson*

Top left: SLM-built 2-6-0T E71 out of use at Tua in 1959./*A. Trickett*

Bottom left: 2-6-0T E81, built by Emil Kessler at Esslingen in 1886, waits to leave Tua with the afternoon mixed train up the narrow-gauge branch./*M. J. F.*

Above: A later Esslingen engine to the same design as the E81 series, E111 sets off from the junction with the mixed train in October 1974./*M. J. F.*

Below: Silhouette of E81 near Sendas on the evening Mirandela-Bragança working. /*L. A. Nixon*

Above: 2-6-0T E113 on a Tua line mixed train in the uplands near Bragança. */W. J. V. Anderson*

Right: E112 heading the evening Mirandela-Bragança mixed train over the viaduct at the approach to Jerusalem de São Romeu.*/M. J. F.*

Left: Two of the Esslingen 1889 0-6-0Ts cross at Cachão on the Tua line. E52 is named *Vizeu*, a reminder that the Dão and Tua lines both belonged originally to the *Companhia Nacional.*/*W. J. V. Anderson*

Above: Borsig compound 4-6-0 238 in the Douro gorge between Tua and Alegria, with a Porto-Barca d'Alva train. /*W. J. V. Anderson*

Below: The last of a long and aristocratic French line, de Glehn du Bousquet compound 4-6-0 268, built by Fives-Lille in 1903, was working the Regua-Poçinho mixed above Tua in August 1969./*S. C. Crook*

Top right: Looking up the Douro valley at Ferradosa, with a westbound train crossing the river./*W. J. V. Anderson*

Below right: Inside-cylinder 4-6-0 284 high above the river near Vesuvio. /*W. J. V. Anderson*

Above: The last surviving Beira Alta compound, Henschel 4-6-0 211 leaving Poçinho with the evening mixed train for Regua./*W. J. V. Anderson*

Below: A 2-4-6-0T crosses the road/rail bridge at Poçinho with the Sabor line mixed train for Duas Igrejas, railhead for Miranda do Douro./*G. W. Morrison*

Right: 2-4-6-0T E201 on the Duas Igrejas-Poçinho *misto* near Lagoaca./*L. A. Nixon*

E201

Minor Railways

Above: A view of the installations of the *FC de Mallorca* at Palma, with a Nasmyth-Wilson 4-4-0T shunting./*B. A. Butt*

The *San Feliu-Gerona* line was a 750mm gauge line linking the town of San Feliu on the Costa Brava with the city of Gerona. *Right:* 0-6-2T No 4 (Krauss, 1890) is seen leaving Gerona with an evening train. *(E. F. Bentley)*. *Below:* No 5 on a morning train in more rural surroundings./*P. W. Gray*

These two views of the *Olot-Gerona* metre-gauge line show 2-6-2T No 23, built by MTM of Barcelona. *Above left:* On the turntable at Amer. (*W. J. V. Anderson*). *Below left:* En route to Gerona near Angles./*M. J. F.*

Above: The 600mm *Guardiola-Castellar d'en Huch* line was operated by the cement company Asland. Its industrial nature can be seen in this picture of Orenstein and Koppel 0-4-0WT 11 on a mixed train./*L. King*

Below: Some of the steam stock of the metre-gauge *Catalanes* system inside the shed at Sallent. Prominent is 2-6-0 + 0-6-2 Garratt 106, built by St Leonard in 1925 and allocated to the Manresa-Olvan section./*P. W. Gray*

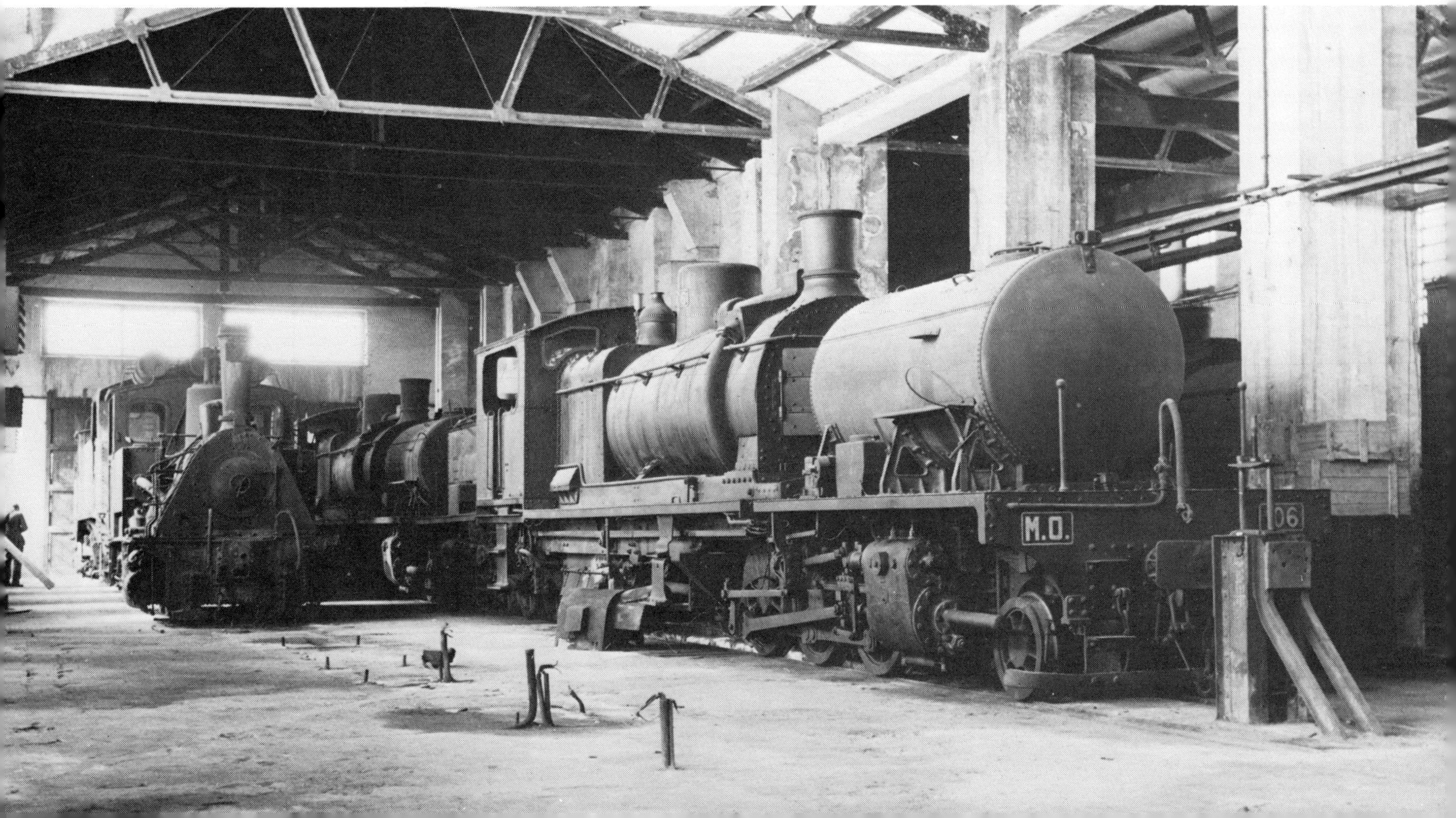

The *Andorra-Escatrón* railway is a broad-gauge line opened in 1953 to connect coal mines at Andorra in the province of Teruel with a power station at Escatrón on the Ebro, some 20 miles away. It is operated by ENDESA. *Above:* Jung 4-8-4T *Andorra* nears Andorra on empties. *Below:* Secondhand Baldwin 2-6-0 No 1 transfers the empties to the colliery./*M. J. F.*

The 750mm gauge *Onda-Castellon* railway was distinguished by its passage of the main streets of Castellon de la Plana. *Top right:* Krauss and Hohenzollern 0-6-0Ts 3 and 9 double-head a train away from Castellon harbour. *Bottom right:* No 9 negotiates a crossroads under the protection of the traffic policeman./*D. Trevor Rowe*

The *Sierra Menera* line was a metre-gauge industrial railway no less than 125 miles long from iron ore mines in the Menera mountains to Sagunto steelworks on the coast. The major gradient was the climb out of the valley of the Rio Turia at Teruel to Puerto Escandón, since this was against the loaded trains. *Below:* NBL 4-8-0 Nos 4 and 7 claw their way up to Escandón with a portion of an ore train. (*M.J.F.*).

Above: Avonside 0-6-0T 205 La *Vascongada* shunts at Gilet./*P. Ransome-Wallis*

Right: 2-6-2 + 2-6-2 Garratt 502 banks a train out of Teruel./*P. W. Gray*

S.M

Nº 4

Left: North British 4-8-0 4 *Juanita* of 1906 assists sister *Isabel* out of Teruel on the *Sierra Menera* line./*M. J. F.*

Two views on the metre-gauge *Carcagente-Denia* railway. *Above:* Dereliction at Corcagente. *(M. Dunnett). Below:* A Franco-Belge 0-6-0T and Black Hawthorn 4-4-0ST outside the shed, the latter dating from 1882./*J. R. P. Hunt*

Left: The interior of Gandia roundhouse, on the *Alcoy-Gandia* railway, contained a *Villena, Alcoy and Yecla* Chemnitz 0-6-0T as well as the AG's own Beyer-Peacock 2-6-2Ts in 1967./*P. Ransome-Wallis*

Below: Estrategicos y Secundarios de Alicante 2-6-0T No 3 en route from Denia to Alicante near Gata./*P. Ransome-Wallis*

Right: JOP (Harbour Board) No 2 at Huelva. /*L. G. Marshall*

Below right: On *Union Explosivos-Rio Tinto's* lengthy mineral line, 3ft 6in-gauge RSH 2-6-0 201 moves an empty ore train through the marshy suburbs of Huelva./*L. A. Nixon*

Right: Apart from Robert Stephenson and Hawthorns 2-6-0 No 201, built in 1953, there are many other hallmarks of the company's British origin in this scene at Rio Tinto.

Bottom right: RSH 2-6-0 200 near Las Mallas, on the 50-odd mile Rio Tinto-Huelva line.

Below: Dubs 0-6-0T 47 of 1881 on a rare main-line working — an enthusiast-catching special organised by the stationmaster at Las Mallas./*L. A. Nixon*

Above: Also on the 3ft 6in gauge, *Buitron-San Juan del Puerto* No 16, a 1908 Barclay 4-6-0T *San Cornelio./P. W. Gray*

Top right: A St Leonard 0-10-0T, No 10 *Calatrava* of SMMP, shunts at one of their mines near Puertollano./*L. A. Nixon*

Below: No 3, *Terrible,* an ominously-named broad-gauge 0-6-0T built by Baldwin in 1901, shunts for ENCAR near Peñarroya. /*W. J. V. Anderson*

Bottom right: On the 750mm gauge *Valdepenas-Puertollano* railway, Orenstein and Koppel 0-6-0 No 6 *Asturias* halts at Calzada de Calatrava./*D. Trevor Rowe*

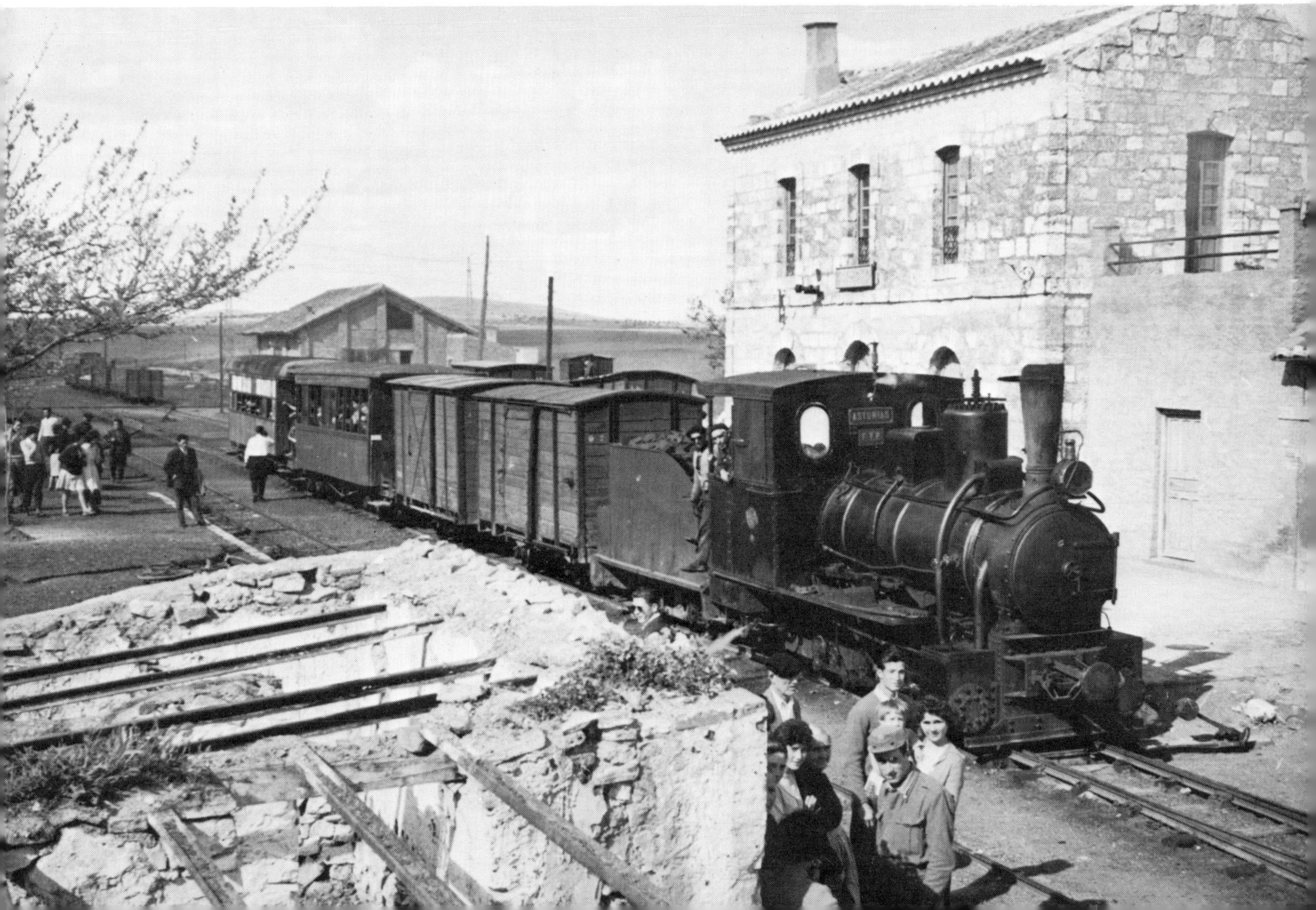

Above: Madrid (Goya) station was the terminus of the metre-gauge *Madrid-Almorox* line. Here Krauss 0-6-0T *Guadarrama* of 1890, numbered as *Madrid, Navalcarnero, Villa del Prado* No 2, waits to leave./*N. N. Forbes*

Below: On the metre gauge *Castilian Secondary Railways* (FSC) an MTM 2-6-0T heads a mixed train towards Medina de Rioseco./*W. J. V. Anderson*

With 212 miles of route along the southern feet of the Cantabrian mountains from Bilbao to Leon and La Robla, the *FC de la Robla* is one of Spain's most notable metre-gauge lines.

Top right: Alco 2-8-2T 60 is entering La Vecilla on the Mataporquera to Leon stopping train. *(L. G. Marshall). Bottom right:* The major passenger power of the *Robla* was a series of SACM Pacifics acquired from the Tunisian Railways. In this scene 184 is leaving Cistierna on train No 1, the La Robla-Bilbao mail.
/*P. W. Gray*

F-R
184

Above: A Baldwin 2-8-0 of 1900, 53 *Valmaseda* shunts at Valmeseda in 1960. /*M. J. F.*

Top right: No 13, Sharp Stewart 2-6-2T *Valderruéda* pulls into Olaveaga on the 06.40 Cidad Dosante-Bilbao./*P. W. Gray*

Below: Another secondhand *Robla* import, 2-6-0 102 *Ceferino de Urien,* was built by the Swiss Locomotive Works in 1902 for the *Rhaetischebahn.*/*P. W. Gray*

Bottom right: It goes without saying that the *Orcanera Iron Ore Co Ltd* was a British project, as witness one of their metre-gauge Beyer-Peacock 2-6-0STs./*D. Trevor Rowe*

ATENCION
AL
TREN

Above: At Babcock & Wilcox's Galindo Locomotive Works, Bilbao, their spare shunter was steamed for the Industrial Railway Society in May 1974. The engine is 0-4-0WT Maffei 4195 of 1925./*M. J. F.*

Left: Inside the Sestao steelworks site of *Altos Hornos de Viscaya,* AVH No 16, an 0-4-0WT by Kerr Stuart, was working on the same day of the IRS visit./*M. J. F.*

The *Sestao-Galdames* mineral line, of 3ft 9in gauge, was initially a British enterprise and retained the original equipment until its recent closure. *Above right:* Kitson 4-6-0 No 7, built in 1874, leaves Sestao with a mineral train in 1969. *(I. K. Samson). Right:* A view of Sestao with a Manning Wardle 0-4-0ST./*P. W. Gray*

The *Santander-Bilbao* railway was a link in the chain of metre-gauge lines ultimately stretching along the Biscay coast all the way from the French frontier to El Ferrol del Caudillo, on the extreme north-west corner of Spain. *Above:* Dubs 4-4-0T 103 *Marron* built in 1896 enters the Concordia terminus at Bilbao, which the SB shares with the Robla. *(P. Ransome-Wallis). Below:* Modern BW 2-8-2T 94, *Augusto La Justicia* runs into Traslavina on a Santander to Bilbao freight. */P. W. Gray*

Top right: Another *Santander-Bilbao* Dubs 4-4-0T, 109 *Bilbao* approaches Santander with a train from Lierganes.*/L. G. Marshall*

Bottom right: The *FC Astillero-Ontaneda* had running powers into Santander over the SB. A06 *Penagos,* a 2-6-2T built by MTM, heads out of Santander in October 1957.*/R. K. Evans*

S
B

AO
Nº6

Left: Metre-gauge 0-6-0T 7 *Reyerta* (Krauss 1913) of *Nueva Montana Quijano* outside their steelworks near Santander./*I. K. Samson*

The next major stage, from Santander to Oviedo was provided by the *FC Cantabrico* as far as Llanes, and the *FC Economicos de Asturias* from there onwards. *Below: Cantabrico* Krauss 2-6-2T No 10 *Cabra* entering Rudaguera on the Oviedo-Santander *correo. (L. G. Marshall). Right: 2-6-0 Turujal*, a Krauss engine articulated to its tender on the Engerth system, waits at Torrelavega with a Santander-Oviedo train./*R. K. Evans*

Below right: 2-4-0T FC 4 *Nansa* built by Dubs in 1894, was the *Cantabrico's* station pilot at Llanes./*M. J. F.*

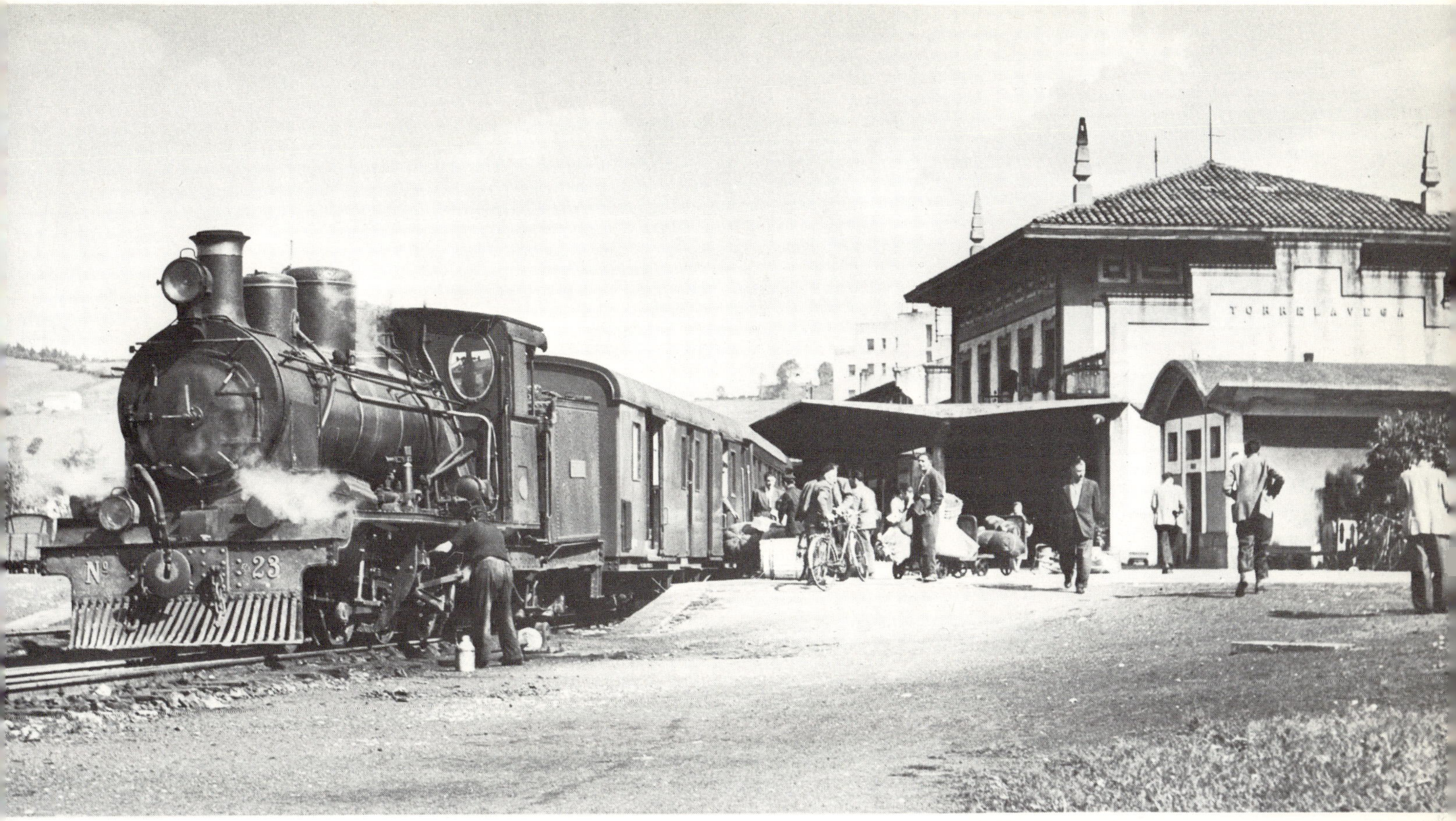
Nº 23
TORRELAVEGA

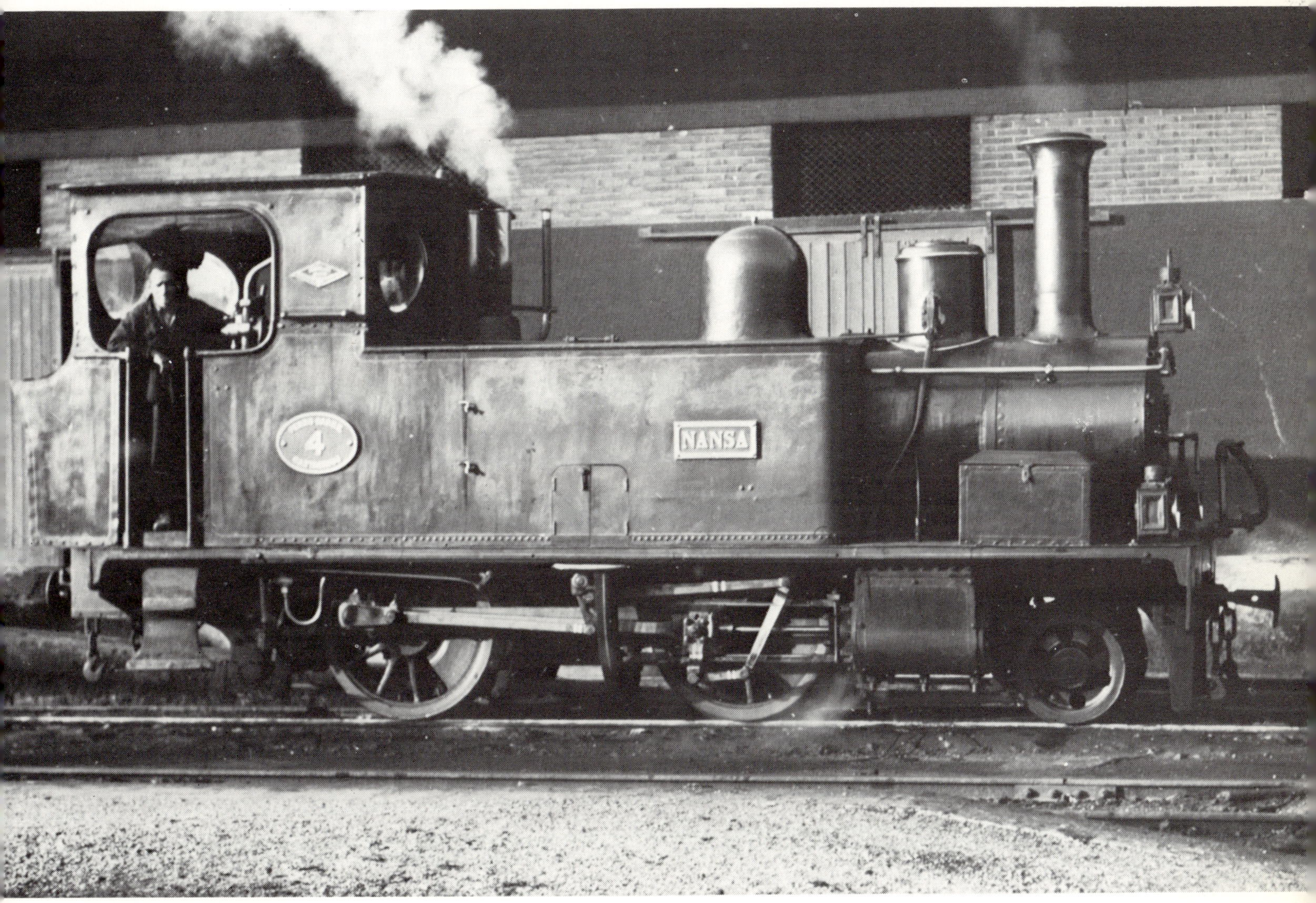
NANSA
4

Above: The Solvay Company operated a coalmine near Lieres, and their Henschel 0-6-0T No 2 is seen approaching the junction with the *FC Economicos./M. J. F.*

Top right: Metre-gauge lines radiating from Oviedo are worked by the *FC Vasco-Asturiana.* In this view of the VA's Oviedo station, Krauss Engerth 2-6-0s 18 and 19 wait to leave for San Esteban and Moreda respectively. */P. W. Gray*

Below: In steam days the *Economicos* was noted for the fine finish of its locomotives, to which Borsig 2-6-2T No 24, built in 1904 testifies./*L. G. Marshall*

Bottom right: A broad-gauge 0-6-0T built by Babcock and Wilcox in 1944 for the Musel port authority seen in 1971 with a train for Aboño./*I. K. Samson*

V.A Nº18
V.A Nº19
Nº10

Control of the collieries around Oviedo is now vested in *Hulleras del Norte, SA,* and in 1974 their Santa Ana complex at El Entrego was still served by steam locomotives of three different gauges. *Below:* The broad-gauge shunter at Carrocera washer was an 1881 Esslingen 0-6-0, RENFE No 030-2418, originally built for the *Asturias-Galicia-Leon* railway. *Right:* A few hundred yards away, *Langreo* BW 0-6-0T 45 was handling the standard-gauge traffic, and Borsig 0-4-0T 27 *Marques de Bolarque* was standby engine on the 650mm gauge. *Bottom right:* 650mm gauge Borsig 0-4-0T 26 *Pilar* arrives at the washer with coal from one of the nearby mines./*M. J. F.*

Nº 27
45

The company *Carbones de la Nueva* built a delightful 650mm gauge line to serve their mines at Samuño, connecting it with the town of Ciaño. These two 1974 views show: *Above:* No 6, Henschel 0-4-0WT of 1927, running a train of colliery tubs down through Samuño. *Left:* No 4, built by Krauss in 1909, commencing the return journey from Ciaño with empties./*M. J. F.*

Above right: The *FC de Langreo* was one of the earliest Spanish railways, and the only one featured in this book to have been built to standard gauge. Its hilly route incorporated inclined planes which were not bypassed until the 1960s. Here, Haine St Pierre 0-6-0PT 26 marshalls a passenger train on to the foot of La Florida incline./*L. G. Marshall*

Right: Another 1974 scene, this time at *Fabrica de Mieres,* where only the coke ovens were still in use at this former steelworks. ENSIDESA 308, a Dubs 0-6-0T of 1891, was shunting wagons on the broad gauge./*M. J. F.*

Nº 26

V 75
HUNOSA
120

HUNOSA

Top left: HUNOSA 120, shunting the screens at Turon, is 0-6-0T built or rebuilt at Turon in 1931./*M. J. F.*

Bottom left: HUNOSA 0-4-0T 38 built by SMDF in 1954, seen shunting at San Andres on the narrow-gauge system formerly connected to Turon./*I. K. Samson*

The *FC Ponferrada-Villablino* is the last wholly steam-operated Spanish metre-gauge system, having 48 miles of track serving collieries and power-stations in the Sil Valley, as well as providing a passenger service. *Above:* 1919 Baldwin 2-6-2T 4 *Ortiz Muriel* pilots an Engerth 2-6-0 19 on a coal train at San Andrés. *Below:* Another Engerth 2-6-0 18 heads a train of empties near Paramo del Sil./*W. J. V. Anderson*

Above: 2-6-2T 7 and Krauss 2-6-0 17 double-head a coal train between Toreno and Cubillos.

Below: Macosa Engerth 2-6-0 14 drifts down from Cubillos with the 15.30 Villablino-Ponferrada *correo./L. A. Nixon*